GOLD CURE

GOLD CURE

TED MATHYS

COFFEE HOUSE PRESS
Minneapolis
2020

Coffee House Press books are available to the trade through our primary distributor, Consortium Book Sales & Distribution, cbsd.com or (800) 283-3572. For personal orders, catalogs, or other information, write to info@coffeehousepress.org.

Coffee House Press is a nonprofit literary publishing house. Support from private foundations, corporate giving programs, government programs, and generous individuals helps make the publication of our books possible. We gratefully acknowledge their support in detail in the back of this book.

LIBRARY OF CONGRESS CATALOGING-IN-PUBLICATION DATA

Names: Mathys, Ted, 1979– author.
Title: Gold cure / Ted Mathys.
Description: Minneapolis : Coffee House Press, 2020.
Identifiers: LCCN 2020002843 (print) | LCCN 2020002844 (ebook) |
    ISBN 9781566895811 (trade paperback) | ISBN 9781566895897
    (ebook)
Subjects: LCGFT: Poetry.
Classification: LCC PS3613.A829 G65 2020 (print) |
    LCC PS3613.A829 (ebook) | DDC 811/.6—dc23
LC record available at https://lccn.loc.gov/2020002843
LC ebook record available at https://lccn.loc.gov/2020002844

Printed in the United States of America
27 26 25 24 23 22 21 20   1 2 3 4 5 6 7 8

CONTENTS

Ring Cycle

GOLD CURE

EL DORADO

El Dorado

With $18 cash, an Igloo cooler
    and a compulsion to name,
7 miles beyond Muddy, population 100,
    7 miles before Equality, population

unknown, through vaporous rain
    falling gently like the Dow,
of sound mind and sound eyes
    in the Year of the Rooster,

on a township road straight as a nail,
    in work boots rubbed with mink oil,
past an irrigation lake, a big-box
    trampoline park, and FREE GOLD

estimates at the pawnshop,
    around a buckle in the slow Saline,
through the illusion of consensus,
    asking nothing of the trees, in daylight

savings, in memory of poetry,
    armed with syntactic categories,
prepositional and hungry,
    I arrive in Eldorado, downstate Illinois.

•

The City of Daffodils has no daffodils.
    It has Dad's BBQ, and Dad is a pig.
His perverted smile is painted on plywood,
    his overalls embroidered with *Dad*.

Dad holds a pulled-pork sandwich
    in his hoof, a cannibal or fractal.
A couple in Carhartts fiddles on iPhones
    over catfish and pickle spears.

Coke comes Regular or Big 32.
    The server's green headband
sprouts two boingy antennae,
    the terminus of each

occupied by a plastic shamrock
    and a mini pot of gold.
I remember it's St. Patrick's Day.
    LIVE WELL, LOVE MUCH, LAUGH OFTEN

says the sign over the booth,
    an admonition that Eldorado
needs no voice-over
    to pin it together like a rivet,

that the kingdom of images
    has its own conquistadors
who arrive in boats that fly no flag
    to fire gild decrepitude into booty

in a complex alchemical process
    that ends in a clean getaway
leaving locals to inhale
    residual mercury vapor.

                    •

So I leave, just another
    Pizarro fixing to return
from the rain forest basin
    to face public opprobrium

with no gold or cinnamon
    to show for looting and torturing
my way through an empty legend,
    my provisions gone, men starved,

indigenous conscripts with smallpox,
    the donkeys sick and the barge rotten.
But I run into road construction
    on the road to Equality. A man

in a neon, knee-length raincoat
    leans on a Caterpillar backhoe
with a sign that says SLOW.
    So I double back to Eldorado

in my little raft of credulity.
    An oil pump in the field
nods up and down approvingly.
    Inland gulls forage at its base,

scattered like grains of wedding rice.
    A deal on oxygen and acetylene
at the hardware store. A square
    of particleboard on the church lawn

gives a blank pixel to Google Earth.
    The digital billboard at Eldorado Spirits
offers video poker and 7-7-7 on the slots,
    gold coins spinning like ballerinas

in egregious pirouettes.
    On the town hall steps
a pair of wet, abandoned gloves.
    One glove points to a plastic marquee

framed by burnt-out bulbs.
    It is as empty as a thought bubble
above a cartoon explorer.
    I fill it with three thoughts.

•

The first is that the boy
   who ditched these gloves
now pumps the pedals of his Huffy
   down a streak of asphalt by the library,

fuel-injected with the dysphoria
   that he has just spent one slow afternoon
in a room with spars of golden light
   tracing the soft floss of his friend's pubic hair

and now might be going to hell.
   The second is that the railroad hand,
who two centuries prior climbed a ladder
   to paint the town name on the depot,

refused to let the town founders,
   Samuel Elder and William Reed,
claim this hinterland as property,
   so changed *Elder-Redo* to *Eldorado,*

an act of fake news with a paintbrush
   that cleaved the sky in two, not east
to Appalachia and west to the Rockies,
   but back to Emperor Atahualpa

strapped in the garrote,
   having forfeited to his executioners
a ransom room of gold ingots,
   and forward to a place name

on the smartphone map app
   my blue dot wanders like a lab rat.
The third is that Eldorado
   was a sundown town. A welcome sign

hung until 1980, warning black citizens
    to depart by dusk. When the pastor
of the African Methodist Church
    was given 24 hours to disappear

under penalty of death,
    he shouldered his shotgun
and dared the mob to make him,
    but a century later the couple

who adopted a biracial child
    woke to sewage slathered
from front porch to mailbox
    where the red flag had been raised.

                    •

The three thoughts recede
    into window paint at Beck's Drugs:
ELDORADO HIGH SCHOOL!
    GO BIG GOLD! BEAT THOSE BULLDOGS!

Since I'm a Spaniard in my first encounter
    with unfamiliar society, my cosmology
won't allow me to believe the gold
    displayed in public is the entire supply,

so I push inside, toward a hidden cache
    under pretense of vitaminwater.
Orthotics, wheelchairs, bariatric
    adjustable beds, Dr. Scholl's,

an aisle of Hallmark cards,
    a cooler of Monster Energy drinks,
clear plastic prescription bags
    hanging neatly in rows

from a system of trellises,
    each like a chrysalis, the Ambien
and Valium, Lithium and Prozac,
    Celexa, Lexapro, Paxil, Cymbalta,

waiting to flex and flutter
    their powdery wings
through all those synapses.
    It is dusk. It is dawning

on me that the golden empire is gross
    exaggeration, that I came
not for the appleness of an apple,
    but the appleness of *this* apple

now refusing to disclose to me its core.
    But between the Rx In and Rx Out
consoles, a TV livestreams a gilded room
    in a distant city, where the gilded one

is about to give a presser. The camera
    idles on its tripod, the frame occupied
by floor-to-ceiling golden drapes
    that shimmer on the plasma screen.

•

Because opening the treasure chest
    always disappoints, I leave
before the microphone goes live.
    At a farm on the periphery,

a horse noses at a midcentury
    truck chassis. A goat lifts her head.
On the way out of town
    I pass a white hearse.

Goldfish

Sometimes a ping-pong ball
ricochets in the improbable

honeycomb of fishbowls—lip
lip—before rimming out

and you are grateful to physics
for saving you from having to

adopt a distressed carnival pet
and send your child off

on her first slow
pilgrimage to grief.

But sometimes a package deal
leaves you stuck with a full

bucket of balls. You put a little
English on a throw, and the wind's

sorcery provides a direct hit,
the splash unnerving the skittish

creature your child declares
is a girl named Marvin.

Eighty dollars later
Marvin is in an aquarium

on your child's dresser
darting in all that water,

all that LED light. Sometimes
diagnoses of shock proliferate

for one who no longer recognizes
the system in which she lives—

lack of appetite, bottom sitting,
black spots, skin flukes, a decline

from golden sheen to sallow white—
until a protective impulse grows

animal in your core. Sometimes
there's a protest on the radio

when you enter your child's room
to retrieve her ladybug rain boots

and find your spouse in her bathrobe
sitting on the bed alone, watching Marvin

swallow a descending flake,
and there's no need to ask why.

Voyager

Digging for vinyl
   in the Goodwill dollar bin
I discover a record
   called *Poet's Gold.*

Produced midcentury
   by RCA, it has Yeats
and Kipling,
   Keats and Millay,

recited with pomposity
   by a tenebrous voice.
When sleep resists,
   I implode on the sofa

and listen to poems
   through pop and hiss,
time and dust.
   I imagine what

I would have included
   on the other golden record
launched by NASA
   the year of my birth.

Millennia after I'm dead
   the golden record will pass
within a light-year
   of an obscure constellation

shaped like a giraffe
   to pose an interpretive problem
to another intelligence.
   Poet's Gold fades

into silence like a thesis
    and the golden record drifts
away from me
    faster than sleep,

but its problem of audience
    lingers: to include laughter,
a dictator, whale song, or "hello"
    in fifty languages?

To notate in the grooves
    Beethoven,
a hydrogen atom,
    to diagram a fern?

If my brain waves were recorded
    would I have the discipline
to conceptualize devotion,
    and to what ideal, or would the EEG

register associative leaps—
    how the sound of a knuckle
cracking under water
    is the click of an electric fence

like the one I stood behind
    while a man I'd once known
put down a sick cow
    with a sledge to the skull,

how the arc of his swing
    was that of an ax
bisecting firewood
    propped up on a stump,

its two halves newly
    exposed to each other
and falling away
    in opposite directions

like a gunman from the kick
    and the victim from impact
or my head to this cushion
    and a record to the stars.

Gold Cure

I claim to destroy only the craving.
          —Dr. Leslie Keeley, 1896

In the story of syringes there are those that give,
those that draw, and those whose hypodermics
contain a serum that is not prophylactic

but therapeutic, a double chloride of gold
injected twice daily at the Corn Belt sanatorium
into arms of incoming inebriates and opium eaters,

sots from Chicago, the jiggered and boryeyed,
habitués of hashish, arsenic, ether, and though
the doctor's proprietary tonic is cut with morphine,

willow bark, ammonia, and cocaine,
Keeley was the first to treat booze as disease.
And if I am given one wooden coin

to drop into the time-travel slot,
I'll escort my father to one of Keeley's
franchised institutes, maybe Cincinnati.

We'll ride the train across the Ohio line
from wherever we are or were, sunlight warming
our upholstered berth. We'll use what little time

we have left to laugh at the story of his granddaughter
giving the glowering phlebotomist one hell of a time,
knotted on my lap in tears and hyperventilation

like Laocoön strangled by snakes, refusing to forfeit
her blood to a lead test. My father will be in a suit,
his breath between mouthwash and ingested vodka

as he tells me the story of hitchhiking to Alaska
to pan for gold but getting drafted, of mowing down
a water buffalo he mistook for footsteps with his M-60

after dark. I'll split my tolerance from my tolerance,
thank him for his temperance during my youth.
From the station we will stroll an avenue

alive with cyclists and flittering sycamore leaves,
joking about how we're both in good spirits.
Through the welcome gate we will assume

chaise lounges by a fountain and submit
our left forearms in parallel, like an equals sign.
Keeley will say, as he prepares our syringes,

that if alcohol is the genius of the gambling den,
it is also the emblem of blood at the Lord's Supper.
If it is crime, it is also sacrament. If it is poison,

it is also medicine. Our needles then will sink in.
I'll close my eyes and embrace gold in my veins.
Synthesized in the collision of neutron stars,

thrown down in asteroids, the gold resists
my earthly physiology. It passes through me
like wind through a screen, leaving only

a vague remainder, this dull glow—
hard to locate in the body—that aches
for an answer just out of reach.

When I open my eyes my father will be gone,
of course, his suit folded on the chaise.
That is how this phase of life goes.

The wind will have eased. Keeley will eye the suit
as if to say that, like the eye of a cyclone,
the period of sobriety was part of the disease.

Fool's Gold

This morning I love everyone,
even Jerome, the neighbor I hate,
and the sun. And the sun

has pre-warmed my bucket seat
for the drive up Arsenal Street
with the hot-car effect,

a phenomenon climatologists
use to explain global warming
to senators and kids.

I love the limited edition
gold Swingline stapler
in the oil change lounge,

which can, like a poem,
affix anything to anything
on paper. One sheet of paper,

for instance, for that cloud of gnats,
one for this lady's pit mix
wagging his tail so violently

I fear he'll hurt his hips.
One sheet for glittered lip balm,
for eye contact, Bitcoin extortion

and the imperfect tense.
Sheets for each unfulfilled wish
I left in a penny in a mall fountain.

Sun spills into the lounge
through the window decal
in geometric Tetris wedges.

I have a sheet for Tetris,
its random sequence of pieces
falling toward me in this well

like color coded aspects of the life
I neglected to live, for the pleasure
of making line after line

disappear. The gold stapler
has a twenty-sheet capacity
so I straighten my stack

on the reception counter
and staple the day together
with an echoing *chunk.*

Melt Value

To be worth my weight in gold
at the going price of gold
I'd need to be a gnome,
knee-high, dense, with mass
equal to the body weight
I had when I had words.

I'd be a golden nude,
my feet shrunken to stubs,
arms brushed to soften
their luster, sunlight
striking my abdomen
in a steady candle flame.

Only my face would be polished
to high gloss, a gnostic
expression lost in my eyes
behind the death mask
of Tutankhamun.

I'd be a period piece
displayed in a glass vitrine.
You might come to me
in the museum's final hour
and ask my form to answer for
a melt value that made us both.

Or I could be large,
life-sized, but hollow.
Hammered into sheets
I'd be soldered into a man
impervious to fire, alloyed
with palladium, posed midlife
in midstride in a sculpture garden.

I would throw sun
back at the sun. My open
palm would shine, smooth
where the life line should be.
But I'd need, in my dark interior,
a nest of wire and steel
to prevent my heavy trunk
from slumping into itself.

You might visit me there
on a tour, in a certain
subjunctive mood,
reading in the brochure
a story about a story
about who I might've been
and why I'm still in transit
to a city I'll never reach
that therefore never was.

A Raft of Rushes

It matters only that it floats.
In one origin story
it is a log boat. A dugout
in another. In the version
the New World chronicler
writes for Old World financiers,
rushes are cut from shore
around the crater lake
and lashed into a raft.

But accounts of the ritual itself
are consistent as a dream
within the European dream:
the chief is alone in a cave.
No chili, salt, or sunlight.

He walks out of the mouth.
They roll him in turpentine,
powder him with gold dust.
He loads emeralds, pendants,
resin, gold bracelets, oblations.

He pilots the raft of rushes
to the center of Lake Guatavita,
off-loads treasure to water
and paddles back to shore.
Children set the raft on fire.

One rush burns for Fernández de Oviedo in the wake of
    Conquest, who claimed to have witnessed the ritual;

One rush for Rodríguez Freyle, who rehashed de Oviedo's
    account, calling the chief *el dorado,* the gilded one;

One rush for Marcos de Niza, who boasted of seven cities of gold;

One for Coronado, who found only a pueblo;

One rush burns for Columbus pacing the Pinta, anchored
between a rocky islet and a reef as natives paddle away, gold
studs in their noses and calabashes sloshing with freshwater,
writing *Should I meet with gold or spices in great quantity,
I shall remain till I collect as much as possible, and for this
purpose I am proceeding solely in quest of them*;

One for Ponce de León, who died of thigh wounds en route;

For Sepúlveda, enslaving 8,000 laborers to drain the lake for
emeralds, breastplates, eagle and serpent artifacts until the
cliffs collapsed killing all, one rush burns;

One rush glows hot for the golden plaza of Cuzco;

Two for Pizarro, one the elder, one the younger, the latter gone
astray on the Napo River, blaming the fiasco on a village of
Amazonian women raining arrows on the barge;

One rush flares up for Quesada disfigured by leprosy, one for
Benalcázar, and also Philipp von Hutten;

One burns for Sir Walter Raleigh after Roanoke and the Virginia
Colony, on parole from the Tower of London, going south for
El Dorado and ending up beheaded;

One rush each for Cripple Creek, the forty-niners, and Fort Knox;

One rush burns for Mark Twain before fame, prospecting in
Nevada, shaking quicksilver from a buckskin sack onto the
amalgamation pan, packing the pulp into snowballs, the gold
ring he forgot to remove disintegrating on contact;

Rushes burn for the gold standard, golden ratio, and the golden
hour when the sun is lowest, reddest, softest, throwing the
masted ships into silhouette.

KEY TO THE KINGDOM

Key to the Kingdom

—July, 2016

This is the key to the kingdom, rustproof
nickel silver, cut by a man in uniform
in the hardware aisle on a rotating steel
carbide blade, a vise securing the blank,
the key's rounded bow a medallion of sun
with a hole punched through to hang
on its galactic ring. Weightless in the palm,
the shoulder is sharp to mark the exact
depth of engagement. A jagged range
of peaks garnish the shaft, align
with wards in the pin tumbler keyway
and unlock the door, swung open to reveal

the kingdom. Of rain, of infancy, kingdom
of clapboard, concealed carry, of the night shift
at Frito-Lay, nuclear gerontology at Los Alamos,
L-shaped couches, tributaries of heroin up
the Mississippi basin, of prison writing workshops,
kingdom of arugula, of a slaughtered peewee team
invoking the mercy rule, peaches and asters, of
helicopter cinematography, a girl blowing bubbles
over the river, of a poet unable to sustain
the Blakean conviction that all subjectivities,
predator and prey, are holy, that police are,
a coyote stalking the pinnacles, a bald eagle at the zoo.

In that kingdom there is a state, the state
with the prettiest name, land of flowers
on the conquistador's tongue, the state of
brackish water, coastline, and glade, made
habitable by sugar and central air, porn mecca
with oranges, flakka zombie flail, grandchildren
lollygagging in manatee exhibits, space exploration
over a red tide in the cape east of the *polis*
where a dance club pulses until a man
enucleates its love. If blinded by hatred
of those unlike himself, or by hatred of himself,
the stem that anchors the thorn is the same.

In that state there is a city in its morning thaw,
flag over the courthouse at half-mast, a hollow
sidewalk yawning to accept boxes of granola,
olives, wheels of manchego slid down into
the deli's larder, newspapers slung at stoops
from a crawling minivan, women in yoga pants
clutching Lululemon mats like scrolls, diesel exhaust,
certified nurses in scrubs issuing into the hospital
where a man bleeds from a hole in his still-
uncertain future and a woman veers into labor,
the ovaries in the fetus in her womb already freighted
with all the egg cells her child will possess.

Over that city there is a forecast, severe weather,
a storm that hangs like a decaying gourd from twine
in the kingdom's portico, gourd of a variety present
in the New World before Columbus, the exact moment
of its breaking impossible to predict but certain
to arrive when its curved neck can no longer
sustain the weight of its own rot and snaps, drops,
blows open nutty white flesh on steps below,
gale force and hail wrung out of the jet stream's
trough and bulge contact zones, over grasslands, then
south to the city where white men confuse any threat
to their absolute power as a form of persecution.

In that storm there is a house, its roofline lashed
by rain that courses down asphalt shingles
to decorative gables, slides over dormers,
pools in gutters, then runs down downspouts
onto the saturated lawn, water wrapping the house
like a body in muslin. A house in old colonial style
but thrown off by additions in the back, interior walls
subtracted for flow, a decade-by-decade replacement
of hardwood floors, fixtures, the chimney sealed up,
molting over generations each original element
like the ship of Theseus, this poem of slow violence
with bodies that change in a form that remains.

And now that she is at rest, poor woman,
now that the sky's ritual errancies have tried
to sack her house and failed, and fled,
Justine is alone again. A black kerchief
tied across her eyes, she measures in darkness
ground coffee beans, strong as rocket fuel,
on a digital scale, pours steaming water in ovals
to bloom the beans. When the brew is rich
and viscous, she glides to her typewriter and writes
"In that house there is only this room."
She removes her sword from the wall
and cuts the blindfold from her eyes.

In that room there is a bed, Justine's bed,
tucked with hospital corners, quilt spread
tight as a drumskin and depicting a black cross
side to side, toe to head, marking the kingdom's
epicenter in crosshairs beneath which she slept.
The bed is empty. Justine is gone. She drags
her sword through thick woods, alive with new
perceptual acuity, hacking at brambles, hoverflies
mobbing her head as she reaches the brook, blade
glinting with orange flecks of sunset as she writes
the word "retribution" in the sky, leaving tracers
in her vision like a sparkler on the Fourth of July.

On the bed Justine left behind, there is a book
bound in leather, the one that wrote her into allegory
long before statues in her honor were erected
in civil squares, dog-eared at the passage in which
she is still an ideal, standing blind in train tracks
with a falcon on her shoulder. Before she sees
the locomotive, she hears the bell, bell, bell,
feels the ties tremble and then the engine's
pistons announcing the arrival of freight: an eight-
ton BearCat armored personnel vehicle, assault rifles,
Kevlar helmets, pilotless surveillance drone, hounds of hell,
bomb-disarming robots, and 400 sworn officers of the law.

In the final pages of that book there is a flowering plant,
blue false indigo, native to America, growing wild
at the border of the forest where Justine now stands,
its roots described as woody, black, unkillable, branching
underground in a rhizomatic hydra of power belonging
to no one, to all, its genus derived from the Greek,
bapto, as in dip, immerse, baptize, and make new
from criminal soil. In writing, the plant is motionless,
an image that flickers in the mind and recedes again
into the grammar of its making, but in the wind
that wraps Justine just now, the plant is stereoscopic,
gray-green leaves waving, violet flowers in riot.

In that plant there is a sap that goes blue
on contact with oxygen. It contains a toxin.
Toxic blue dye comes alive as Justine slices
into the hairless stem. Silken weapon,
it beads then streams toward her heels, a blue
the Greeks could not see, blue of the ribbon
holding back Washington's hair, blue robin's egg
cradled in the nest, blue of the officer's uniform
the moment before he raises his firearm, Neptune's
blue glow, blue of her birth certificate, and a darker
blue passport embossed with the kingdom's gold eagle,
one talon for the olive branch, one for the arrows.

In that blue there is a belief
that the kingdom's dome has been sealed
from within, that the exceptions have devoured
the rule, that the watchers need to be watched
and the charges dismissed, that the presumption
of safety has been put on permanent layaway
for those not born into it, a presumption replaced
with this color that cuts, as it has, as it must,
both ways. Justine's eyes ache. The sky
is bright with exhortation. She fills each vial
like an inkwell, clambers over monster ferns,
and heads to the city to face the king.

Belief in the blue, in its cruel illusion
of *habeas corpus,* of "You may have a body."
Blue in the sap, in its toxin of last resort.
Sap in the plant, blue false indigo,
its deep and communal roots. Plant
in the book where Justine's an ideal.

Book on the bed in the room she fled
for the city, where if you stand, if you run,
if you resist or comply, where if your pants
are low or high, where to be visible is to hang
in the balance. Bed in the room, room in the house
where she cut the kerchief from her eyes.

House in a storm mistaking its temporary
force as permanent weather, storm in the city
where Justine follows a river of others
into the teargas plume. City in the state
with the prettiest name, state in the kingdom
that forgot its key and kicked in the door.

EL DORADO

The Leprechaun Trap

The instructions for the monthly
kindergarten family project
are vague: *For March,*

make a leprechaun trap.
In the grainy example photo
sent home in her unicorn backpack,

a shoebox decked with aluminum foil
is propped up by a Popsicle stick
over a coil of gold Mardi Gras beads.

The child will pull a length of yarn
tied to the stick when her prey
caves to desire and wanders inside.

If the assignment has pedagogical value
it is not to warn the child against vice,
because a leprechaun is a leprechaun,

but to compel her to spend quality time
with her parents on a project that inducts
her into the adult regime,

where success requires manipulation
of corrupted little men
through acts of imagination.

We settle on a mason jar filled with gelt
left over from Hanukkah. To lure
the leprechaun inside, she twists

a stepladder from pipe cleaners.
Red step, yellow, green step, blue.
It rises to the rim and curls over.

When the leprechaun ascends
her rainbow to the summit,
he will pause a moment in awe

and horror, the surge of impulse
saying *yes,* the weight of experience *no.*
When he cannonballs into chocolate gold,

he will land in a heaven
that is also prison. He will laze
against glass for a solitary night

in the elementary school hallway
amid radiators softly clicking
and three-dimensional book reports.

Bingeing on gelt, stuffing gold foil
wrappers into his satchel, he will be
the bearer of his own subjection

until sunrise, when the chocolate ends.
Belt buckle loosened, stovepipe hat in his hands,
he will pace in circles, warbled chatter

flooding the jar, his walls semitransparent,
admitting light but no clarity, except
for the hole above, in view, out of reach.

This makes her sad, she confesses,
and I agree. But he will have no regrets
because he does not make decisions;

he is a condition. And to succeed,
her trap must make her feel
the purgative power of tragedy.

Plus, I tell her as we wait for the bus,
there is no such thing as leprechauns.
I know, she says, I already know.

Gold Donkey

—Cripple Creek, Colorado

The canary in the gold mine
spent her nights above ground
and days 1000 feet down
the same cool shaft
I descend in a metal cage
to the crosscuts and drifts
blasted into Independence Lode
and hung in her little cage
low between ore-cart wheels
where she could die sacrificially
in an updraft of monoxide.

But the donkey in the gold mine
was born down here, and her
mother before her, a lineage
accustomed to hauling rock
with flecks of quartz and gold
through blackness interrupted
only by a candle strapped
to the mucker's hat
or a calcium carbide lamp
hot with acetylene flame
that leapt at the wind of a sledge,
burnt off a tenderfoot's eyebrows
and singed a black star
into the donkey's hide.

A politician legislated light
into the donkeys' lives
but the asses kicked like mad
when the nippers—kids
at 5 cents a shift—strung them
from the cage's base in slings

and sent them up the shaft
into sun they'd never known.
Like all good ideas, this one
burnt out the retinas in seconds.

While I'm below, a sunset above.
I rise along a wall of oxidized iron
the color of tobacco spit, emerge.
There are twelve donkeys at large
in town, the bartender says, direct
descendants of those from below.
I search for them for an hour
but find only a coyote trotting
the Family Dollar parking lot.

In rain, in the donkeys' honor,
I choose from the strip of casinos
the Brass Ass, wade through
the usual sad cases to roulette.
At the only game with no strategy
my only job is to bet on black, odd,
and constellations of birthdays
then wait like an ass for the house
to place the dolly and rake my chips.

The dealer spins the ball
against the spinning wheel
and sweeps her arm to end all bets.
The bottled water I ordered arrives.
The brand is Eldorado. The ball falls
into 29 black. I win hundreds.
When a donkey bucked and contorted
hard enough to slip free on ascent
it plummeted like a bullet reversing
to explode in its own chamber.
Chips in stacks float to me on felt.
They are not gold but powder blue.

Path of Totality

For two minutes
and thirty-seven seconds
in a shadowed band that stretches

coast to coast,
all the gold on earlobes,
collarbones, and fingers

given in promises,
remembrances, and gifts
to those arranged on blankets

with cardboard solar glasses
pressed to upturned eyes
is valueless in darkness.

Gilt Frame

In the university administration hall,
past Admissions, in a recess easy to miss,
where Jesuits once performed an exorcism

on an adolescent host who spoke in tongues,
hang a small Renoir and a smaller Chagall,
dully glowing, uneven with the floor.

I correct the Chagall with the back of my wrist,
afraid to touch the artwork, a spectral nude
emerging in white from a charcoal lake.

How easy would it be to lift the frame
from the wall, the glass from the frame,
the drawing from the glass, the figure

from her lake, the soul from its establishment,
two dimensions from three. But gilt possesses
executive authority, and my hand withdraws.

Both over- and understatement, the frame's
style is a vehicle to amplify its scene
but also to harmonize with its surroundings,

to disappear into the architectural idiom
of Renaissance Florence, a container contained
between control and withdrawal, exorcism in reverse.

The longer I stand the more I desire
to steal the frame and discard the Chagall,
to run my fingers over the frame's

recurring motif of leaves and scrolls,
rusticated flower heads, chiseled from linden
by an artisan with a single tool,

wood chips snowing onto her boots,
her squirrel tail brush dipped in water to slick
the frame, sheets of gold leaf too thin to handle

applied to wetted wood with a gilder's tip;
to run my eyes over the absence where art was
and my concentration over a plan

to smuggle the frame from the admin hall
zipped in my jacket, to hold it up
to the photo-realism of traffic,

elevate it for a falling leaf to enter red
and exit with an aureate glow,
to hang the frame around my neck.

Utopia

The gold toilet is utopian.
24-karat-plated, installed
in a unisex alcove
restroom at the museum,
it is open to one patron
at a time. I wait in line.

The only part about Duchamp
that interests me anymore
is his chess career, but I know
his *Fountain* brought us here,
a century late, to a gallery guard
yawning through his spiel
about how the gold commode
(his term) is fully functional
and titled *America.*

A woman wielding
an audio tour wand
disappears behind the door
into Sir Thomas More's
Utopia, where ideal citizens avoid
the corrupting influence of gold
by forging it into chamber pots
and chains for criminals.

The woman emerges
expressionless as a dinner plate,
wand hanging at her hip
like a sword. The guard
invites me to enter
into a space of reflection
with the piece, to use it "regular,"
and keep my eye on the time.

Duchamp anoints the abject,
More profanes the precious,
each of them an archer
shooting an arrow up
in a parabolic arc. They cross
midair over this horseshoe seat
gleaming in museum light.
My inability to relieve myself
is a failure of art, or a failure
to imagine myself as part
of an ideal society.

Into the purgatorial
latticework of cast-iron pipes
I flush the artist and philosopher
where they join with effluent
from hotels and theaters,
grease from griddles, water
from affluent brownstones,
power-washed windows
in the Diamond District,
runoff from Columbus Circle.

Outside *America*, I find Picasso's
Woman Ironing, early Blue period,
its gaunt laundry worker
with an angular shoulder,
a proletarian emblem
pressing her flat iron
into a scrim of fabric
on the gray-white table.

Scholars believe the painting
hides another, earlier portrait
that the artist abandoned
of a smug man upside down
wearing a red bow tie,

his face compressed
beneath her iron's weight,
his privilege effaced
in the reclaimed surface.

King of Roses

I am the barber to the King of Roses.
Back from the bower he sprawls in my chair.
He removes his hat and lets down his hair.
It cascades around his donkey ears.

Velvety dun, they pop up like horns.
I've signed a nondisclosure agreement.
I work my lather and ready my blade.
I'm like a post to whom he talks.

He divested himself of the golden touch.
Washed it off at a bend in the river.
Then he took an oath against stupidity.
But there's always a story after the story.

Always a competition in need of a judge.
He was the judge between satyr and god.
There's always a god with a fragile ego.
If you ask me, you side with the god.

But a king does not consult a barber.
Now my employer is a bank of shame.
Tonight I will dig a hole in the field.
I will speak his secret into the dirt.

All winter long I'll give him his trims.
Reeds in spring will sprout at my spot.
Stirred by wind, the reeds will whisper
The monarch will listen if you rip off his hat.

Gold Dredge

—Sumpter, Oregon

Fog-white, bulky as a five-story factory,
the dredge is shipwrecked in its own pond.
Atlantis, not sunken but abandoned.

I lean on a railing in the winch room.
A bead of sweat drips from my nose
to an acquisitive minnow that flashes

to greet it. The pond is ringed by *dead men*:
pines and firs to which cables were stretched
to steady the hull from bow and stern.

For decades it crawled, pivoting on its spud
as the buckets gnawed through acreage,
digesting rock in the swirling trommel,

flushing the slurry through sluices,
dragging its pond along as hostage,
pausing for war and resuming again

with an increase in the price of gold,
leaving a trail of tailings down the valley
like the path of slime behind a slug.

Dead men are reflected in the water
that the boilers thawed each winter.
A blossom blown from a stalk of mullein

disturbs the surface tension.
The pale figure of the Dredge Master
ripples in the syntax of minnows.

His smile widens to silent laughter
as he raises a wooden riffle
caked with black sand and heavy metals.

He lifts his tongue to flash me the gold coin,
spit-slicked and placed there after his death,
a small denomination to pay the ferryman

to pole him across the river in a skiff.
A wildfire high in the Elkhorn Mountains
has burned for days. The advancing mass

of smoke and ash wraps the foothills
and slides through stands of dead men
like an exhalation after long-held breath.

SHALE PLAYS

Lessons learned can be shared and modified from play to play, [but] each one has distinct properties which require custom approaches in order to maximize gas and oil recovery.

—Halliburton

oh, yes, yes, the matter goes on, // turning into this and that, never the same thing / twice: but what about the spirit ...

—A. R. Ammons

Bakken

FRACKN8R and BONEASS write their names
on their helmets in Sharpie. The chainhand
flips the bird to the egghead in the data van.
Land rights and mineral rights separate

in Nodak's split estate. The blackboard's blackness
is hydrocarbon in shale. A roan horse goes
diarrheal. Man camps get real. Injection wells
induce seismicity but the wages make fracktivists

jealous. The pressure differential is like opening
an airplane window at 30,000 feet. BONEASS:
You just spud the well and it bubbles right up.

Custom says pinholes on the red wellhead valve
point north. Derrickman climbs to the crown.
The prairie's small fires flare all around.

Anadarko

Let plankton, symmetrical as filigree metalwork,
die. Before the dinosaurs, beneath the inland sea
between Appalachia and Laramidia, let its silica
cell walls inter the afterlife of sunlight, work down

the water column, phosphorescent in thought,
black in the actual. Under pressure, let desire
descend, sift with deep marine snow, and reside
on seafloor mud 300 million years before

Comanche County, Oklahoma. Repression,
the analyst writes, shelters that which is intolerable
to the conscious mind, and would, if released, create

tremendous anxiety. Good anthropomorphist I am,
plankton's lonely down in the play. Bad apologist I am,
a pocket of sunlight sings from the black hurray.

Barnett

Tray tables up. On final approach, STL to DFW,
she points out from her big-girl seat in 24E
a discolored pixel in the quilt below. No, Sweet Pea,
that's not a Tower of Control. It's a frack pad. What you

can't see is the Octopus of Boreholes beneath the rig
flexing in eight directions under the Dallas metroplex.
Octopus secretes his slurry of ink to extract a halo effect:
cheap gas, distillates, cheap plastics, your Legos

and Magna-Tiles made affordable by the fossil angel
exhumed. Laid over. Between Brooks Brothers
and Auntie Anne's in the Junior Flyers' Club,

she removes her shoes. They go in this plastic bin.
She steers a replica baggage car, pilots a plastic Airbus.
The slide is a jumbo briefcase. She goes down laughing.

Fayetteville

Acid scours the wellbore. Water-soluble guar
to regulate viscosity. South to north on US 65,
a fleet of 300 carbon steel tankers is alive
with 400 million gallons of alluvial aquifer.

Poseidon's dominion is both ocean and earthquake
but the Ozarks aren't Greek. During inspection
the farmer's trident pitchfork leans in his barn
while he swallows the lease. The play goes bulimic.

Radioactive flowback is pooled in ponds—
benzene, xylene, naphthalene—spread on fields,
re-injected beneath his rooster's bloodline song.

Three counties away, an Iraq vet with PTSD
braces for the next tremor in a beige La-Z-Boy.
He watches a documentary about the tides and sea.

Eagle Ford

Sweet when she's low in sulfur, *sour* when high,
light when she flows, *heavy* when syrupy slow,
the djinn inhabits an orbit unseen, unknown
until Petrohawk opens the oil window. Fortified

by smokeless fire, her Arabic cognate is *insane*
but she's generous, murderous, neutral, depending.
Petrohawk lengthens her sweet spot, sliding in
his horizontal bit like a mallet finger stained

with gelling agent. In *I Dream of Jeannie* she's half-naked
in pantaloons, rubbed from her bottle by an astronaut
who then serially corks her in sitcom bondage fantasy.

My desire, every episode, is for her to revolt,
afflict him with the skin rash, nosebleed, sore throat,
burning eyes, and vomiting of shale gas syndrome.

Devonian

BCE lightning strikes desert methane vents
and Persians worship eternal fires. In Homer,
the fire-breathing Chimera reverses her
snake tail to ignite her own origin on Mount

Chimaera's rock seeps catalyzed by ruthenium.
In the Torah, seraphim flame. In deep
concentration an Iroquois boy smears shallow
oil on his palms to waterproof his canoe. In *Boom*

Town, Clark Gable's a wildcatter refined by the girl.
In '73 OPEC punishes the U.S. for supporting Israel
in the Yom Kippur War. In '79, diamond-tipped bits.

In '05 slickwater toxics are classified as trade secrets.
In the basement, I do darks in a natural gas dryer
so loud the falcon cannot hear the falconer.

Haynesville

FAUST
    Come in then!
MEPHISTO
    That's the spirit.
              —*Goethe*

88 MPH on a road he knows, no seat belt, no
phantom medical episode, the shale gas CEO
plows into an overpass. Rigged to run on CNG,
his Tahoe explodes. A permanent shadow

sears into ragweed. Afterglow in Riyadh,
in Caracas. The black box captures vehicle
data, but motivation creates an epistemological
crisis. It cannot know that he was indicted

the day before for conspiring to rig leases,
or that NatGas stocks rally on news of his death,
or that eight years prior the Sierra Club chairman,

to depose King Coal, accepted his $26 million
in donations. *Conspire:* to breathe together,
spirit of the *demos* that whispers "come in."

Niobrara

When a pointillist blob of fossil fuel wells
overwhelms my laptop map of the play,
I exit the café and find an actual fossil, gray
trilobite sealed in a decorative pebble.

I take it home for my daughter's terrarium.
It now lives with what else has died but lives
again in glass—a hawk feather, crisp leaves,
a pine cone, a robin's nest, and a freshwater clam

on a bed of ghost-white aquarium gravel.
Some nights, when I come home to a house
asleep, my emptiness fixed on its own completion,

I lift the small lid and run my finger down
the trilobite's washboard segments. I can only
bring myself to do this when all the lights are out.

Marcellus

One of the things I kinda like is my stuff leads to a volatile conclusion.
  —Quentin Tarantino on *Pulp Fiction*

Cinephiles debate the boreal glow
emitted by Marsellus Wallace's stolen
briefcase. A baby nuke, gold bullion,
an Oscar, Elvis's golden lamé tuxedo,

a 60-watt soft-white or Marsellus's soul
extracted from a borehole in his neck,
overlaid with a Band-Aid. Vincent
Vega pops the combination: 666,

luminesces from the contents, later
gets wasted by Butch. But in the diner,
with a .45 in his face, Jules

> flips the locks and opens the case, revealing it to
> Pumpkin but not to us. The same light SHINES from
> the case. Pumpkin's expression goes to amazement.
> Honey Bunny, across the room, can't see shit.
>
> ### HONEY BUNNY
> What is it? What is it?
>
> ### PUMPKIN
> (softly)
> Is that what I think it is?
>
> Jules nods his head: "yes."
>
> ### PUMPKIN
> It's beautiful.
>
> Jules nods his head: "yes."
>
> ### HONEY BUNNY
> Goddammit, what is it?

Granite Wash

The swath of lithologies is shaped like a mitten
knitted around the hand of the past. The palm
blooms in supplication, as if to take alms
or release an invisible methane pigeon

to crosswind. The pigeon banks, flails,
a fugitive emission from the tight-gas basin
in flight from custody, justice, vigilante citizens,
arrest. Convicted in absentia, the bird jumps bail,

detectable only by a thermal camera's spectral
infrared. The force that shot the blossom
through the green fuse drives her pinions

into atmospheric gas. She diffuses. Her wingspan's
global, centimeter-thin, and denied on C-SPAN
as a weather anomaly of hurricane proportion.

Monterey

I hung a walnut in California, cycloptic
in its beaten tree. San Joaquin Valley
gathered up around, orchards of kiwis,
peaches, hay and alfalfa, grapes and garlic

in rows, pistachios, a festival of asparagus.
Its shell a skull, its kernel the folded brain
with no idea of drought or the subterranean
fault. My fault, yours. In the gathering forest

of derricks, the walnut dropped and bounced
economically. Ground to Agra Grit, it was sold
as abrasive blast media to power-spray graffiti

from a mosque, sold as proppant to Venoco
to inject into fissures in shale, to hold them
open for fuel, to find dominion there.

Permian Basin

—for Brooks Miller

As boys, by flashlight, we buried our blood,
a blow dart, and a Kirby Puckett rookie card
in a thermos time capsule beneath your slide.
Now when I call, you're on Pronghorn Road

to a well, to placate a client about the glut:
We clubbed and dragged to the cave more meat
than we can possibly eat. Use-it-or-lose-it leases
left you drilled but uncompleted wells, "DUCS"

you yell in traffic. I want to open our covenant,
but it's not time, you say, because it's not time
we agreed would unearth it, but desire. The poet

I sent you wrote *Who holds the lease on time*
and on disgrace? I'm losing you to static
and DUC, DUC, DUC, DUC, DUC, goose.

Utica

In pink doctor kits, in dolls that urinate,
in parachutist, police car, gunslinger cowboy
with lasso & hat, the philosopher of toys
finds functional homunculi of what adults

fail to find aberrant—incarceration, firearms,
disciplines, disease. Having read his book of myths,
the PR team rolls out a coloring book for kids.
"Talisman Terry, Your Friendly Fracosaurus"

is here to teach you about a clean energy source
called Natural Gas, found here in the Twin Tiers!
Don't worry, Terry wears boots, a safety vest,

a hard hat, and Fracosaurus gloves, and when
the well is complete and your crayons are done,
the land will look the same as before.

Woodford

There is no bridge. Only this shaded interim
where a hernia of sun breaks the canopy
and deposits its coin in the shallow creek.
I've waded in. A red leaf skates up, spins

in circles, a red record, guarding light in veins
like a summation it can't find the energy
to recite. Reddened river. Rubicon. Prophecy
and its affiliate, black market belief that rain

can chaperone the leaf, eddying at my ankle
out of sight. What then to praise, the light,
the leaf, or the water's departure beneath?

There is no bridge. Only sundown recalling
commerce from my hand submerged
in deeper stones I can no longer afford.

RING CYCLE

Ring Cycle

It is time for Mr. Rogers. My daughter settles into my lap. The episode concerns gold and rainbows. Its formal structure is a chiasmus in which we will encounter the rainbow of alloys in processed gold—white gold, yellow gold, rose, green—and the purported pot of gold at the end of each rainbow. Mr. Rogers arrives at the tail end of the initial jingle, inexplicably shining a flashlight on his palm, and gestures us inside.

We speculate that our daughter was conceived on our wedding night, hours after we exchanged rings. Six months prior, on a houseboat in Oregon, I sat before a window wall that admitted the river in panorama. On the far shore, by a pylon's spear-like shadow, a kayaker idled in her red nylon windbreaker, eyeing a cormorant, its wet wings fanned wide to dry in the sun. On her ring finger, gold glinted against the paddle's shaft like a spark. On the screen between us, I priced wedding rings.

In the foyer closet Mr. Rogers breaks protocol, rejects his arsenal of sweaters—red, yellow, green, blue—and slips into a white lab coat. I have no answer when my daughter asks why. Now I see the white coat as metacinema, a spectrum before it is scattered, a color that contains all others, white of sunlight, milk, snow, his lab coat reproduced on the TV screen with RGB modeling, the red, blue, and green projected in overlay to make my daughter's eyes and mine perceive white, a rainbow of sweaters collapsed into one.

We wanted gold for both wedding bands or for neither, some symmetry as emblem of the long song to which we didn't yet know the lyrics. But the internet said we could afford only one in gold, so we forfeited symmetry to budget, and mine arrived, months later, in a fist-sized box from Philadelphia, in sterling silver.

Mr. Rogers guides us to the kitchen, where we're going to make a rainbow with his flashlight and a spray bottle. He fills the bottle at the tap and squirts a fine mist, through which he projects his beam. No dice. His second attempt also fails. No rainbow on the cabinet, Mr. Rogers is crushed. He calls Mr. McFeely for assistance.

During the first month of marriage, we developed a modified, slow-motion fist bump in which our rings met with the muted click of soft metal on soft metal, the way two people tacitly agree after years of texting that a particular emoji works as private code for *I hear you, we're good.* Her ring is now the only pure gold in the house, which demotes the dog-eared books, kitchen knives, faded sofa pillows, and IKEA lamps into a ziggurat of chintz. But when my silver clicks against her gold I hear our contract sealed in a golden mean, that felicitous middle between excess and deficiency that Aristotle positions not as an average but as balance, prerequisite to beauty.

It is alarming to see Mr. Rogers so enraged by his failure at craft rainbowing. In the living room, he retrieves a pad of butcher paper and takes fat crayons to it with the meditated violence of Cy Twombly in the Trojan War series. At this, my daughter heaves her weight into my chest as if we're launching in a space shuttle, her legs tense in their jeggings. "There are things you can do when you're angry," Mr. Rogers mutters as he executes a crayon rainbow on the paper like a scythe. Afterward, sitting in the bowl of zen that follows his discharge of adrenaline, he regards his rainbow. "Rainbow," he says. He pats the rainbow. "You know, it really is scary when you're angry. You just don't think you're able to stop."

Some equate the Goldilocks fairy tale with Aristotle's golden mean, but this misreads the *Nicomachean Ethics*. Because Goldilocks employs a dialectic decision tree—porridge too hot, porridge too cold, porridge just right, chair too big, chair too small, chair just right, bed too firm, bed too soft, bed just right—we are tempted to think she has arrived at virtuous pragmatism, rejecting extremes and therefore denying both vices and false ideals. But evaluating Goldilocks in this way misses that her ethics is circumscribed wholly by the world of the absent bears' possessions, that she's a materialist whose dramatic need is pillage. Aristotle's golden mean requires continuous acting in accordance with virtues like happiness that are desired for themselves, not for the material rewards they provide. The just-rightness of the porridge is neither just nor right. Perhaps this is why, in the original, Goldilocks is an old, foulmouthed vagrant named Silver Hair who falls while fleeing the bears and breaks her neck.

Months after the ceremony, in winter, we took our honeymoon in the Virgin Islands. Her sky-blue two-piece had become a navy-blue one-piece; she had started to show. She left me under a palapa and waded tentatively into the sea. As each swell approached she spun, hands on abdomen, allowing the wave to break against her back. On this sand the U.S. Navy conducted live training exercises, ship-to-shore gunfire, air-to-ground bombing, amphibious landing drills. The historical no-go zone left the beach pristine. Earlier in the day we'd seen a rainbow, but now a squall dominated the horizon. Small against heaving water, she was out where a marine would have surfaced and charged the ghost enemy on shore, and before, where Columbus wrote to the crown *their Highnesses may see that I shall give them as much gold as they need . . . and slaves as many as they shall order to be shipped.* She waved from the water. There was no sun to make out her ring.

Mr. Rogers retrieves his royal-blue castle from the shelf in the kitchen and sets it on the table. The screen quavers, and we enter the Neighborhood of Make-Believe. King Friday is holding a contest, called "Draw the Neighborhood of Make-Believe." He's announced that the prize will involve many colors. Lady Elaine sings "I'm going to win, I'm going to win" and shows Neighbor Aber her contest entry, a painting on a red boomerang. The recto is a self-portrait, the verso a rendering of her kaleidoscopic museum-go-round. "You can tell King Friday I'm ready to win the prize," Lady Elaine preens, "which is all the gold in the world." Neighbor Aber is puzzled. "Mmm-hmm," Lady Elaine says, "the king said the prize would be many colors, so I think it's going to be all the gold in the world."

The morning Margaret Thatcher died I woke in jail. In an orange jumpsuit with no possessions but my socks, I was on a thin mat on the rubberized floor with twenty others. It was 5:00 a.m. I was hungover, which is why I was there. Still at a conference, my spouse was asleep on a friend's futon in Brooklyn, my daughter asleep inside of her. An officer threw Nutri-Grain bars at us from the doorway. "Breakfast!" A raspberry one hit me in the chest. My neighbor wanted to trade. Along the wall a man sucked violently on his right ring finger, down to the knuckle. Was he gagging himself? Later he yelled "hah!" and spat out his gold wedding ring, transferred it back to his left hand. He must have switched it before booking because his right knuckle was bigger than his left. Must have told the officer he'd have to sever his finger to remove it. His saliva was the recovery mechanism. Now he had his ring, and mine was hanging somewhere in a vinyl inmate property bag with my pants. Time to talk to the judge on a TV screen. She asked, "Have you learned anything?" "Yes, your honor, I have."

King Friday assembles the neighborhood for judging. He hopes for rain. "What's all this about rain," Lady Elaine says. "I don't want rain unless it's raining gold." Hypnotized by the episode, my daughter absent-mindedly munches a bowl of Goldfish. Their form is fish-like but not species specific. Each has a tail fin, ovoid body, an indentation for an eye, and a dopey smile (The Snack That Smiles Back). Pepperidge Farm prints the features only on one side of the Goldfish, suggesting they actually may be flounder. Flounder are born with one eye on each side of the head, but as they grow one eye migrates over the dorsum to join the other. They are camouflage experts that lie on the seafloor, peering up with both eyes to predators droning above. I ask my daughter for one of her Goldfish. She says no. In the snack aisle I once tried to buy her a box of exotic, multicolored Goldfish, a rainbow of Goldfish, but she refused with militancy.

King Friday awards the prize to Ana Platypus. Lady Elaine is livid. The king concedes that Lady Elaine's entry was moving, but Ana won because her drawing included people. Lady Elaine screams that hers also included a person, "me . . . the winner!" Yes it did, the king agrees, but Ana's included *everybody*. Because this is Make-Believe, the king expresses extraordinary social vision. The health of the kingdom requires collectivity. And in awarding the prize to a platypus, a semi-aquatic, egg-laying mammal with a duck's bill, a beaver's tail, and an otter's fur, the monarch affirms the intersectional nature of the ideal neighbor.

At protests my daughter rides on my shoulders, from which she conducts surveillance and points out costumes. At a march downtown, the organizers turned right toward the river, rather than left as the permit required. My daughter saw red-and-blue lights before I did, asked why they were putting the man inside the car. At the intersection the crowd formed a circular ring around the squad car and sat down en masse. My daughter sat crisscross applesauce and asked why we were sitting in a ring, like morning meeting at school. After twenty minutes of chanting "Let him go! Let him go!" my daughter watched the man exit the squad car. "I'm glad they let him go," she said.

"The prize is for you, Ana," King Friday says, "but really it's for *everybody*." What the hell is Ana going to do with all the gold, Lady Elaine would like to know. The prize is many colors, King Friday explains, but it's not gold. Lady Elaine digs in: "I hope it's a truck delivering all the gold, that's what I hope." The neighbors look skyward. The prize is a rainbow on a rainless day. Ana Platypus is delighted to share it with all. Lady Elaine is having none of it. She announces she's leaving to find the rainbow's end. She has become a conquistador. "You can have the rainbow," she says, disappearing beneath the curtain to start her expedition. "I will have the gold."

The first conquistador was Jason, who led the band of Argonauts in their quest for the Golden Fleece. He was sent on a suicide mission to an island where the fleece hung in a tree, guarded by a terrible serpent. The king of the island had a daughter, Medea, who possessed powerful magic, magic that Jason brutally manipulated to survive. A pawn in a squabble between gods, Medea was pierced by Cupid's arrow, evacuating her dark knowledge and replacing it with manic passion for Jason. The king had set up a series of impossible tasks for Jason to complete in order to get the fleece, obstacles that would surely kill him. Medea could betray her father and help Jason, or betray her passion for Jason and be miserable. After writing off suicide, she starts to make plans.

Emei Shan, in western China, is one of the country's nine sacred mountains. One can summit via a thirteen-hour hike up stone steps through bamboo forest to icy switchbacks among pilgrims who bow down and touch their foreheads to every step, or a minibus ride up the back side of the mountain. When I arrived, exhausted by the hike and my ridiculousness, I was above clouds. At the lookout a street performer stood with a monkey on his shoulder. It was spray-painted gold and leashed to his belt loop by a small chain. I stepped to the platform edge. As an optical phenomenon, a rainbow is a half ring, but in theory a rainbow makes a complete circle if viewed from a position where sun through water vapor is unobstructed by earth. Because it rises above clouds, Emei Shan has full-circle rainbows. I looked down into one. The prior year the authorities had erected a safety fence to prevent any more pilgrims from committing suicide by diving through the circular rainbow in pursuit of eternal life.

Medea inoculates Jason with ointment derived from Prometheus's blood. He starts in on his gauntlet. After he yokes bronze-hoofed, fire-breathing bulls and plows the plain, after he scatters dragon teeth like seed in the furrows and sees the teeth sprout into warriors, after he follows Medea's counsel and throws a stone into the scrum of weapons and flesh, causing the warriors to murder one another, after Medea sings the serpent that guards the golden fleece to sleep, after Jason retrieves the fleece, Medea finds herself at what screenwriters call the *crisis point*. A climax can make fireworks in the plot, but a crisis is the more vital moment when the forces set in motion by the film can no longer be reversed, when the protagonist faces an impossible choice. Medea has ruled out suicide and betrayed her father, but she knows that Jason has the gold and when he returns home he'll abandon and humiliate her.

The screen wobbles again. Mr. Rogers is consistent in signaling transition back from Make-Believe. My spouse joins us on the couch. I eye her gold ring. She eats a few of our daughter's Goldfish and gets scolded. Mr. Rogers directs us to the painting on his living room wall, a reproduction of Seurat's *A Sunday Afternoon on the Island of La Grande Jatte* in a gold frame. The painting transforms into a screen within our television screen, showing a film about gold processing. We ride an ore cart through a tunnel, watch rocks on conveyor belts get pulverized and mixed with water. "It takes 6,000 pounds of rock to make an ounce of gold," Mr. Rogers says in voice-over. Molten rock cascades like lava. "People pour the liquid gold into a mold. A mold for gold!" disembodied Mr. Rogers says with delight. A worker in a blue jumpsuit pulls a gold bar from the water and strokes it with his palm like a wet fish. "And it is known," Mr. Rogers says, "as a good delivery bar."

When we fight, neither of us can fall asleep until we've reconciled. Neither can stand to go get some air like in the movies. When one of us has accused the other of gaslighting, it takes even longer to sniff out who has consolidated power by making the other question their reality. We wander our lightless tunnels of indignation until eventually they intersect in a muted click of silver ring on gold ring. "You just don't think you're able to stop," Mr. Rogers said, "but if you find something *to do* that doesn't hurt you or anybody else, it really can help you feel better." Medea never does feel better. She flees her father, joins Jason on the boat, murders and dismembers her brother, throws him into the sea to distract her pursuing father, convinces two daughters of one of Jason's enemies to kill their own father and boil his body parts in a vat, murders Jason's new wife with a poisonous gown, murders her own sons to save them from slavery, then departs to the clouds in a chariot staffed by dragons. The sky holds no rainbow.

Mr. McFeely arrives to help Mr. Rogers make his rainbow, with Guard Aber in tow. Mr. Rogers is fidgety, impatient to get on with it, until he learns Guard Aber has brought a briefcase of gold. He produces a velvet bag and slides samples of yellow gold, white gold, green gold, and pink gold into his palm, each the size of a salon-grade artificial fingernail. The three discuss the quixotic desire for gold at the end of the rainbow, how the ephemeral pleasure of witnessing a rainbow in the company of others is more valuable than a private cache of indestructible gold. But then Guard Aber hands Mr. Rogers a six-pound gold bar. "Oh, oh!" Mr. Rogers gushes, "I've never felt anything so heavy!" He laughs to disguise his evident pleasure, but the moment feels extra-diegetic; not even Fred Rogers is immune.

Mr. McFeely has brought a prism and helps Mr. Rogers make his home rainbow. Mr. Rogers feeds his fish, removes the white lab coat, sings his song. The episode's formal demands have collapsed the real into the unreal, El Dorado into the neighborhood, the rainbow's impermanence into the dream of gold's eternal life. But it offers no moral. I'd like to think my daughter has internalized the terrors of material pursuit or the joy in collective experience. I suspect she's retained nothing more than the irrefutable value of directed anger.

My daughter wants to see some gold. My spouse hands over her ring. My daughter closes her fist and shakes the ring like she's caught a housefly. Then she puts it in her mouth and looks at us with a maniacal smile. "Don't swallow that!" we yell. "Spit it out. Spit it out!"

ACKNOWLEDGMENTS & NOTES

Grateful acknowledgment is made to the editors of the following publications, in which some of these poems first appeared: Academy of American Poets' Poem-a-Day, *Boston Review, Foundry, Ninth Letter, Pleiades,* the *Literary Review,* and *Western Humanities Review.* Fellowships from the National Endowment for the Arts and the St. Louis Regional Arts Commission provided valuable time and support.

For your eyes on these poems and your wisdom, thank you T. J. DiFrancesco, Greg Hewett, Devin Johnston, Dana Levin, Daniel Poppick, Christian Schlegel, Lisa Wells, and especially Rachel Greenwald Smith. Many thanks to Chris Fischbach, Erika Stevens, and the wonderful staff at Coffee House Press.

"El Dorado" uses an anecdote from *Sundown Towns: A Hidden Dimension of American Racism* by James W. Loewen.

"Gold Cure" references the Keeley Cure, developed by Dr. Leslie Keeley and practiced in franchised Keeley Institutes nationwide. Several lines are drawn from Keeley's *The Non-Heredity of Inebriety.*

"A Raft of Rushes" and "Ring Cycle" quote the diary of Christopher Columbus, as transcribed in 1530 by Bartolomé de Las Casas.

"Key to the Kingdom" was written in July 2016, following the Orlando nightclub shooting; police killings of Alton Sterling in Baton Rouge and Philando Castile in St. Paul; the ambush of police officers in Dallas; and the Republican National Convention in Cleveland. The structure is based on an anonymous nursery rhyme of the same name. The poem uses a line from Elizabeth Bishop's

"Florida," and several lines paraphrase interview comments from Marc Lamont Hill.

"Utopia" is after the sculpture *America* by Maurizio Cattelan.

"King of Roses" is a retelling of the Midas myth after Midas has lost the golden touch.

For "Gold Dredge" I am indebted to Jered Bogli.

Each of the sonnets in "Shale Plays" is titled after one of the fourteen major shale plays in the continental United States. I'm grateful to Brooks Miller for providing much valuable information from inside the energy industry. "Barnett" refers to the "halo effect," industry terminology for the way in which cheap natural gas lowers the prices of downstream consumer products. "Devonian" uses a line from William Butler Yeats's "The Second Coming." "Haynesville" makes reference to Aubrey McClendon, CEO of Chesapeake Energy until his death in 2016. "Marcellus" quotes a scene from Quentin Tarantino's screenplay for *Pulp Fiction*. "Granite Wash" reworks a line from Dylan Thomas's poem "The force that through the green fuse drives the flower." "Monterey" responds to Wallace Stevens's "Anecdote of the Jar." "Permian Basin" quotes a line from Hart Crane's "The Bridge." "Utica" references "Toys" in Roland Barthes's *Mythologies*.

Coffee House Press began as a small letterpress operation in 1972 and has grown into an internationally renowned nonprofit publisher of literary fiction, essay, poetry, and other work that doesn't fit neatly into genre categories.

Coffee House is both a publisher and an arts organization. Through our *Books in Action* program and publications, we've become interdisciplinary collaborators and incubators for new work and audience experiences. Our vision for the future is one where a publisher is a catalyst and connector.

LITERATURE
is not the same thing as
PUBLISHING

Funder Acknowledgments

Coffee House Press is an internationally renowned independent book publisher and arts nonprofit based in Minneapolis, MN; through its literary publications and *Books in Action* program, Coffee House acts as a catalyst and connector—between authors and readers, ideas and resources, creativity and community, inspiration and action.

Coffee House Press books are made possible through the generous support of grants and donations from corporations, state and federal grant programs, family foundations, and the many individuals who believe in the transformational power of literature. This activity is made possible by the voters of Minnesota through a Minnesota State Arts Board Operating Support grant, thanks to the legislative appropriation from the Arts and Cultural Heritage Fund. Coffee House also receives major operating support from the Amazon Literary Partnership, Jerome Foundation, McKnight Foundation, Target Foundation, and the National Endowment for the Arts (NEA). To find out more about how NEA grants impact individuals and communities, visit www.arts.gov.

Coffee House Press receives additional support from the Elmer L. & Eleanor J. Andersen Foundation; the David & Mary Anderson Family Foundation; Bookmobile; Dorsey & Whitney LLP; Foundation Technologies; Fredrikson & Byron, P.A.; the Fringe Foundation; Kenneth Koch Literary Estate; the Matching Grant Program Fund of the Minneapolis Foundation; Mr. Pancks' Fund in memory of Graham Kimpton; the Schwab Charitable Fund; Schwegman, Lundberg & Woessner, P.A.; the Silicon Valley Community Foundation; and the U.S. Bank Foundation.

The Publisher's Circle of Coffee House Press

Publisher's Circle members make significant contributions to Coffee House Press's annual giving campaign. Understanding that a strong financial base is necessary for the press to meet the challenges and opportunities that arise each year, this group plays a crucial part in the success of Coffee House's mission.

Recent Publisher's Circle members include many anonymous donors, Patricia A. Beithon, the E. Thomas Binger & Rebecca Rand Fund of the Minneapolis Foundation, Andrew Brantingham, Dave & Kelli Cloutier, Louise Copeland, Jane Dalrymple-Hollo & Stephen Parlato, Mary Ebert & Paul Stembler, Kaywin Feldman & Jim Lutz, Chris Fischbach & Katie Dublinski, Sally French, Jocelyn Hale & Glenn Miller, the Rehael Fund-Roger Hale/Nor Hall of the Minneapolis Foundation, Randy Hartten & Ron Lotz, Dylan Hicks & Nina Hale, William Hardacker, Randall Heath, Jeffrey Hom, Carl & Heidi Horsch, the Amy L. Hubbard & Geoffrey J. Kehoe Fund, Kenneth & Susan Kahn, Stephen & Isabel Keating, Julia Klein, the Kenneth Koch Literary Estate, Cinda Kornblum, Jennifer Kwon Dobbs & Stefan Liess, the Lambert Family Foundation, the Lenfestey Family Foundation, Joy Linsday Crow, Sarah Lutman & Rob Rudolph, the Carol & Aaron Mack Charitable Fund of the Minneapolis Foundation, George & Olga Mack, Joshua Mack & Ron Warren, Gillian McCain, Malcolm S. McDermid & Katie Windle, Mary & Malcolm McDermid, Sjur Midness & Briar Andresen, Daniel N. Smith III & Maureen Millea Smith, Peter Nelson & Jennifer Swenson, Enrique & Jennifer Olivarez, Alan Polsky, Robin Preble, Alexis Scott, Ruth Stricker Dayton, Jeffrey Sugerman & Sarah Schultz, Nan G. Swid, Kenneth Thorp in memory of Allan Kornblum & Rochelle Ratner, Patricia Tilton, Stu Wilson & Melissa Barker, Warren D. Woessner & Iris C. Freeman, and Margaret Wurtele.

For more information about the Publisher's Circle and other ways to support Coffee House Press books, authors, and activities, please visit www.coffeehousepress.org/pages/donate or contact us at info@coffeehousepress.org.

Ted Mathys is the author of three previous books of poetry, *Null Set, The Spoils,* and *Forge,* all from Coffee House Press. The recipient of fellowships and awards from the National Endowment for the Arts, the New York Foundation for the Arts, and the Poetry Society of America, his work has appeared in the *American Poetry Review, BOMB, Boston Review, Conjunctions,* PBS *NewsHour,* and elsewhere. He holds an MFA from the Iowa Writers' Workshop and lives in Saint Louis, where he teaches at Saint Louis University and curates the 100 Boots Poetry Series at the Pulitzer Arts Foundation. For more information, visit www.tedmathys.com.

Gold Cure was designed by
Bookmobile Design & Digital Publisher Services.
Text is set in Questa.